Ocean of Thoughts

**Copyright © 2017
by Sandeep Ravidutt Sharma**

All rights reserved. No part of this book may be reproduced or transmitted in any form or by any means without written permission from the author.

If you have further questions, contact on

Phone: +919969256731
Email: sandeepraviduttsharma@gmail.com

Dedication

This book is dedicated to **Lord Kartikeya** also know by names like Murugan, Shanmukha, Subrahmanya, Kumaraswamy and Skanda. In Hinduism Lord Kartikeya is worshipped as the God of war and victory. He is brave and intelligent leader of God's forces. He is the son of Lord Shiva and Goddess Parvati who was created to destroy demonic forces symbolising negative tendencies in this world.

To please **Lord Kartikeya** praying for the victory and success of my readers in their endeavour, i hereby recite the following mantra...

"Om Saravana Bhava"

© Ocean of Thoughts
BY SANDEEP RAVIDUTT SHARMA

Table of Contents

Foreword I

Ocean of Thoughts..................................1

© Ocean of Thoughts
BY SANDEEP RAVIDUTT SHARMA

Foreword

This book provides you with a list of 100 positive, inspiring and motivating thoughts churned out by my mind with the grace of **Lord Kartikeya**.

I'm sure if you keep reading, referring and sharing these thoughts and quotes, you will draw inspiration and it would motivate you to take your first step forward towards achieving success and happiness in your life.

"Take a dip in the Ocean of Thoughts and find pearls of wisdom and happiness."

I sincerely hope, you will find this book amazing, interesting, rejuvenating, unique and a constant source of Inspiration.

Thank You and Happy Reading.

OCEAN OF THOUGHTS

© **Ocean of Thoughts**
BY SANDEEP RAVIDUTT SHARMA

Fighting for the cause is more important than winning the war.

© **Ocean of Thoughts**
BY SANDEEP RAVIDUTT SHARMA

There is no end to our requirements in life. To live a happy life you need to feel content with what you have. Happiness is a state of mind.

Don't expect or wait for any award for expressing your kindness. Be kind to people and you get blessings as your reward.

© **Ocean of Thoughts**
BY SANDEEP RAVIDUTT SHARMA

Things or people who may appear impressive sometimes turn up the other way round. Impression is no doubt important but the real strength lies not only in your outward appearance but more within your thoughts, deeds and core values.

Don't make fun of the poor. Money doesn't have a permanent address.

© **Ocean of Thoughts**
BY SANDEEP RAVIDUTT SHARMA

Don't blame previous generation about the current problems. Thank them for feeding you to survive and empower you to speak.

It's nice if you forgive deeds of those who have hurt you in some form or the other. The next level is to forget that you have forgiven and behave as if no such thing has ever happened. No doubt it's easy to preach than practice. Try your best.

Real winners share their credits with all those who made the win possible.

We have both positive and negative traits within us. When you have extreme of any of this, it's time to change or culminate into the other. Avoid extremes of both positive and negative attitude and traits. Too much of anything in this world is not desirable and healthy.

Feeling Good itself is an announcement of Sun rise in your mind. Negative thoughts cannot survive during those moment.

© Ocean of Thoughts
BY SANDEEP RAVIDUTT SHARMA

When you have to say... Enough is enough, it means you have already reached boundary line of your patience. You are on the verge of unlearning all good things in life. Only exceptional persons would still maintain their cool even in adversity. Try to keep patience and save yourself from doing something which the other person wanted so that there is no difference left between both of you.

No one can steal your peace of mind unless you allow them in the first place.

© **Ocean of Thoughts**
BY SANDEEP RAVIDUTT SHARMA

Live NOW is not just a slogan but a way of life.

Commit yourself completely either to a cause or a person. Honour your commitment and your honour remains intact.

It's not important to know what you have lost rather remember what you have gained in life.

© Ocean of Thoughts
BY SANDEEP RAVIDUTT SHARMA

Never judge a person just based on their unfriendly behavior. Their outer behaviour may be influenced by their inner turmoil which you may not be aware of.

Moon is enough to fight the battle against darkness

© **Ocean of Thoughts**
BY SANDEEP RAVIDUTT SHARMA

Don't try to find faults in others. Instead look for their strengths and leverage it with your goals.

Expectations are the root cause of all kinds of suffering.

Never hesitate to say what is there in your mind. It helps in quick resolution or reaction.

Emotions affect you more than anything else in this world. Emotions mirror your inner soul. Don't hide your emotions.

© Ocean of Thoughts
BY SANDEEP RAVIDUTT SHARMA

Clouds of opportunity waits for none. Grab it in time.

If you fail, accept your defeat and close the chapter. Don't give excuses or blame others. Prepare for the next innings with double the energy.

© Ocean of Thoughts
BY SANDEEP RAVIDUTT SHARMA

Fill your life with colours of joy. Feel the happiness. Life is beautiful so are you.

If you feel sorry most of the time in your relationship then it's wise to break free.

© **Ocean of Thoughts**
BY SANDEEP RAVIDUTT SHARMA

Music without ears is no music at all.

Never lose hope.

© **Ocean of Thoughts**
BY SANDEEP RAVIDUTT SHARMA

There is no factory in this world which can churn happiness for you. Your heart and mind together can make you happy.

© **Ocean of Thoughts**
BY SANDEEP RAVIDUTT SHARMA

Don't become slave of your negative thoughts. Immerse your mind in rainbow of good thoughts. Thinking in black and white should be reserved only for certain occasions which are beyond your control.

No one has the power to influence you unless you allow.

It's easy to declare war but it's much more easier to declare peace. All you need to do is listen to the others point of view.

Expectations from others is the root cause of rift in your relationship If the focus is on what one has to offer to others. Life would be more meaningful and beautiful.

© Ocean of Thoughts
BY SANDEEP RAVIDUTT SHARMA

Feeling of revenge doesn't help anyone. Forgive and you will be happy.

Expectations should be realistic else it brings pain and sufferings. No expectation helps to perform without any burden and raises the bar.

Accepting mistakes when told can go a long way towards achieving success.

© Ocean of Thoughts
BY SANDEEP RAVIDUTT SHARMA

Don't ever enter into the race for proving your greatness. Great people don't require any proof to show

Sometimes thoughts appear to be random and sequential at other times. Whatever it is...capture your good thoughts and share. Also not every thought is for everyone.

© Ocean of Thoughts
BY SANDEEP RAVIDUTT SHARMA

If you focus on what you have decided, success is not far.

Encourage those who have taken the first step towards progress.

There are times when whatever decision you take ends in a failure. God is testing your patience...so keep trying without losing hope. You are sure to win.

Hope to see the world glowing and peace returning on Earth would need your active contribution.

© Ocean of Thoughts
BY SANDEEP RAVIDUTT SHARMA

Feeling good is a state of mind. Sometimes we may feel good and attribute it to others. But the fact is, it's our own mind which decides whether the feeling is good or bad. So train your own self to draw happiness or good feeling even in adverse circumstances.

© Ocean of Thoughts
BY SANDEEP RAVIDUTT SHARMA

When you meet someone for the first time you may smile, feel comfortable and behave as if this person is known to you for quite a long time. At other times the moment you see someone you are agitated even when no words were exchanged. It's quite natural but seems to be mysterious. It seems we throw bio signals which attract some and repel others....

© Ocean of Thoughts
BY SANDEEP RAVIDUTT SHARMA

Come out of your shell, you are not born to do limited things in life. You have the whole world as your playground. Take a decision to move forward. Life will never be the same again

Wants causes pain and panic. Don't be slave of your wants.

Truth inspires one and all. Make attempt to live a life with truth and honesty.

Real test of your personality can come at any moment. One may lose all kinds of knowledge, virtue of patience and calm behaviour, the moment someone criticises. Anger in a second would destroy all your good traits like a nuclear bomb and for that moment you are a changed personality. Rare are those who would remain calm in all situations.

© Ocean of Thoughts
BY SANDEEP RAVIDUTT SHARMA

No one has the capacity to hide truth forever.

Sun never stops to shine. Why can't we pursue our dreams and shine?

Attracting people can never be the goal of a positive thinker as he is sure positivity ultimately makes everyone happy and binds all.

Life don't give you option always. You need to earn it.

No one else can say, 'I'm happy' on your behalf. Your choices in life has got the power to make you happy or sad.

Just by observing the nature around you. It brings back balance in your life. It's like practicing meditation with your eyes open.

Every now and then you express your wishlist but ultimately God or the creator surprises you with his wishlist for you.

Don't expect kindness from people who trade lives with money.

If you have acted in time, you don't have to give excuses.

Wheel of fortune stops at you only because of your good deeds and God's blessings.

© **Ocean of Thoughts**
BY SANDEEP RAVIDUTT SHARMA

There is no place on this earth and the entire universe where the will and grace of God don't exist. All you need is pure thoughts and complete surrender to the almighty to experience the same.

When a big curtain of problems falls on you. You have got just one option...TEAR...with two different sides to it. One signifies strength and the other indicates weakness. TEAR Apart or Shed TEARS... Choice is all yours...

© **Ocean of Thoughts**
BY SANDEEP RAVIDUTT SHARMA

Enjoy every moment of your life.

© **Ocean of Thoughts**
BY SANDEEP RAVIDUTT SHARMA

Sometimes those who have knowledge start believing that no one can match their abilities. They tend to forget that on this Earth every one imitates what already existed. What one knows today, somebody had known in the past and someone will know in future. Believe in sharing knowledge and shed your eGo of knowing all.

Life can be in minutes, days, months or years. But the fact says it's just one moment after the other.

© **Ocean of Thoughts**
BY SANDEEP RAVIDUTT SHARMA

Sometimes we know more than what is required. And that kills the joy of knowing something or someone unknown.

© **Ocean of Thoughts**
BY SANDEEP RAVIDUTT SHARMA

Hope without deeds is just a dream.

Name your choices and Universe makes it available.

Don't try to control things whose ownership doesn't rest with you.

© **Ocean of Thoughts**
BY SANDEEP RAVIDUTT SHARMA

Where the Sea ends...
Sky begins..

© **Ocean of Thoughts**
BY SANDEEP RAVIDUTT SHARMA

Realise the gain only when you end your innings.

Don't try to make profit out of every thing. Life is not a Profit and Loss account but a Balance Sheet where all your assets and liabilities are listed and it has to tally. Your Karma or Deeds are your assets. Your misdeeds and sins are your liabilities.

© **Ocean of Thoughts**
BY SANDEEP RAVIDUTT SHARMA

Don't try to live someone else's life.

© Ocean of Thoughts
BY SANDEEP RAVIDUTT SHARMA

Live each day one at a time. Every morning commit yourself to goodness and make attempt through out to achieve positive results.

© Ocean of Thoughts
BY SANDEEP RAVIDUTT SHARMA

Don't try to convey those who pretend to be deaf. Speak to those who want to listen or care for you even if they use sign language.

If you face pain and sufferings, don't inhale it inside. Throw away the pain out of your system by marrying positive thoughts with never say die attitude.

© **Ocean of Thoughts**
BY SANDEEP RAVIDUTT SHARMA

It's nice to know about people who are good looking, intelligent, wise, knowledgeable, brave, richest and so on. What matters more is whether you are a good human in the real sense in terms of kindness, compassion and love.

© **Ocean of Thoughts**
BY SANDEEP RAVIDUTT SHARMA

Don't lose sight of your goals in life else you become wanderer.

Just do whatever your heart says.

Sometimes we spend an entire lifetime to find the purpose of our life. Fortunate ones realises it earlier and make attempt to get the most out of their life.

Whether it was path of success is only known, once you reach your destination.

Accept the fact as it is, don't add exceptions to hide your inability or loss.

Don't beg for wealth, fame and luxury. Beg for knowledge, devotion, blessings, forgiveness and kindness not only for you but for the world.

Great characters don't lose patience at all.

© **Ocean of Thoughts**
BY SANDEEP RAVIDUTT SHARMA

Walking alone can make life difficult. It's better to seek company or join others to cover the distance with ease.

© **Ocean of Thoughts**
BY SANDEEP RAVIDUTT SHARMA

Live each moment without a break

Don't wait and depend on Tomorrow. Tomorrow never comes. Live your life now...

© Ocean of Thoughts
BY SANDEEP RAVIDUTT SHARMA

Enjoy the journey of life rather than getting eager to reach your destination.

© Ocean of Thoughts
BY SANDEEP RAVIDUTT SHARMA

Life is not short for anyone. It so happens that we start living our life quite late. Live NOW.

Don't expect judgement to be always in your favour.

© **Ocean of Thoughts**
BY SANDEEP RAVIDUTT SHARMA

If you follow discipline and rules of life at the appropriate time. You can say, 'All is well' When you don't stick to rules, chaos prevails. And the situation turns into 'All in the well' kind.

Whether you are believer or non believer. God will always be there in some form or the other to protect you. God is great...

© **Ocean of Thoughts**
BY SANDEEP RAVIDUTT SHARMA

Committing errors doesn't portray you weak but repeating those errors definitely does. Learn from your mistakes and never repeat them again.

No one can play the song of sorrow or happiness forever.

© Ocean of Thoughts
BY SANDEEP RAVIDUTT SHARMA

When you like or love someone, don't assume similar feelings from the other end. When you live in an imaginary world, it hurts the most and you start blaming other for rejection. Even to draw a line you need X and Y coordinates. Relationship cannot be one sided.

Quick reaction is helpful when it's a matter of life and death situation. Quick decision is not advisable always especially when the subject matter need proper scrutiny and analysis.

Just to save your life don't hang others.

Express your gratitude through your heart and not just by a robotic 'Thank You' statement.

Wheel of fortune turns in your favour only when you are rotating it and not just watching it roll.

Illusion has many faces. It becomes reality if you believe. And reality becomes illusion if you ignore the truth. Both are creations of the Lord. Choice is all yours which one to live in.

Don't try to act smart unless you really are.

Great achievers help others to win.

© **Ocean of Thoughts**
BY SANDEEP RAVIDUTT SHARMA

Don't ever let your optimism die. Always say it will work in place of it may or it won't. When you discuss any subject see that you are brainstorming on the solution rather than blowing up the problem.

www.ingramcontent.com/pod-product-compliance
Lightning Source LLC
Chambersburg PA
CBHW031439210526
45464CB00005B/2259